GW01464748

New CLAIT

Unit 6
Desktop Publishing

Using
Microsoft® Publisher 2003

Release NC026v1

Note:	*Microsoft and Publisher are registered trademarks of the Microsoft Corporation in the US, UK and other countries. Windows 95, 98, 2000 and 2003 and are trademarks of the Microsoft Corporation.*

Published by:
  CiA Training Ltd
  Business & Innovation Centre
  Sunderland Enterprise Park
  Sunderland SR5 2TH
  United Kingdom
  Tel: +44 (0)191 549 5002
  Fax: +44 (0)191 549 9005
  info@ciatraining.co.uk
  www.ciatraining.co.uk

  ISBN 1 86005 214 2

CIA Training's guides for **New CLAIT** contain a collection of structured exercises to provide support for each unit in the new qualification. The exercises build into a complete open learning package covering the entire syllabus, to teach how to use a particular software application. They are designed to take the user through the features to enhance, fulfil and instil confidence in the product. The accompanying data disk enables the user to practise new techniques without the need for data entry.

This guide was created using version *2003* of *Publisher* running under *Windows XP* and uses the mouse to access features rather than the keyboard. It assumes that the computer is already switched on, and that a printer and mouse are attached.

UNIT 6: DESKTOP PUBLISHING - The guide supporting this unit contains exercises covering the following topics:

- Starting and Closing Publisher
- Recognising the Screen Layout
- Using the Task Pane
- Entering Text into Frames
- Saving Publications
- Opening and Closing Publications
- Text Formatting

- Changing Margins and Layout Guides
- Printing
- Working with Frames
- Importing Text
- Working with Columns
- Working with Pictures
- Templates

Visit www.ciasupport.co.uk for hints, tips and supplementary information on published CiA products.

The guide is suitable for:

- Any individual wishing to sit the OCR examination for this unit. The user works through the guide from start to finish.

- Tutor led groups as reinforcement material. It can be used as and when necessary.

Aim

To provide the knowledge and techniques necessary for the attainment of a certificate in this unit using *Publisher 2003*.

Objectives

After completing the guide the user will be able to:

- Recognise the screen layout

- Save, open and close publications and templates

- Insert and edit text

- Format text

- Use columns

- Work with boxes

- Insert and manipulate pictures

- Print publications

Introduction

This guide assumes that the program has been correctly and **fully** installed on your personal computer. However, in *Publisher 2003*, some features are not initially installed and a prompt to insert the *Office 2003* CD may appear when these features are accessed.

Accompanying text and pictures to be used during the exercises is contained on disk. This avoids unnecessary typing or location of pictures and speeds up the learning process.

Publication data that accompanies this guide has been saved to a certain printer. To save delegates any inconvenience, it is recommended that the tutor resave the files to the appropriate printer, before use.

Important Note For All Users

The disk accompanying this guide contains data files. The user should copy the data into a folder on the hard drive of the computer. Keep the master disk safe and **ALWAYS** use the copied data.

This guide cannot be copied without the permission of CiA Training Ltd.

Notation Used Throughout This Pack

- All key presses are included within < >, e.g. **<Enter>** means press the Enter key.

- Menu commands are written, e.g. **File | Open**.

- The guide is split into individual exercises. Each exercise consists of a written explanation of the feature, followed by a stepped exercise. Read the **Guidelines** and then follow the **Actions**, with reference to the **Guidelines** if necessary.

Recommendations

- It is suggested that the user adds their name, the date and exercise number after completing each exercise that requires a printed copy.

- Accompanying publications for the exercises are contained on disk. This avoids undue typing and speeds up the learning process.

- Read the whole of each exercise before starting to work through it. This ensures the understanding of the topic and prevents unnecessary mistakes.

- Some fonts used in this guide may not be available on all computers. If this is the case select an alternative.

Publisher 2003   New CLAIT

Section 1

Fundamentals

By the end of this Section you should be able to:

Start Publisher
Using the Task Pane
Create a Blank Publication
Recognise the Publisher Screen
Use Text Boxes
Zoom In and Out of a Publication
Close Publisher

Exercise 1 - Starting Publisher

Guidelines:

Publisher is a desktop publishing program, which helps create impressive publications with very little hard work. Each item within a publication, e.g. a picture or a text box, is known as an **object**.

Objects can be moved around and changed to create various effects. The methods used to move, resize or format each object are the same, so once they have been learned, complex publications can easily be created.

There are numerous ways to start *Publisher 2003* depending on how the computer has been set up. The following exercise describes the normal method for starting *Publisher*.

Actions:

1. Click **start** to show the list of **Start** options available. All *Windows* applications can be started from here.

2. Move the mouse to **All Programs**, then over **Microsoft Office** and then over **Microsoft Office Publisher 2003**.

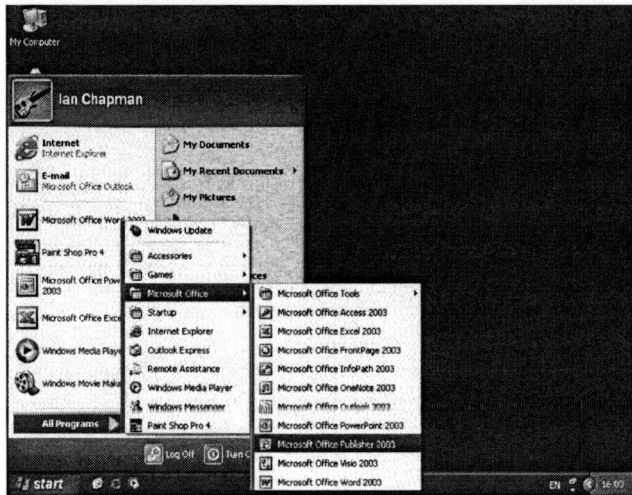

3. Click **Microsoft Office Publisher 2003** to start the application.

Exercise 2 - Using the Task Pane

Guidelines:

The **Task Pane** is *Publisher's* way of helping you create a **publication** – the universal name for the finished article. There are numerous templates available to use. A **template** is a ready-made publication that requires only the text to be edited or may be a picture to be changed, resized, etc.

Actions:

1. When *Publisher* is opened the **New Publication Task Pane** is revealed.

Task Pane

Category list

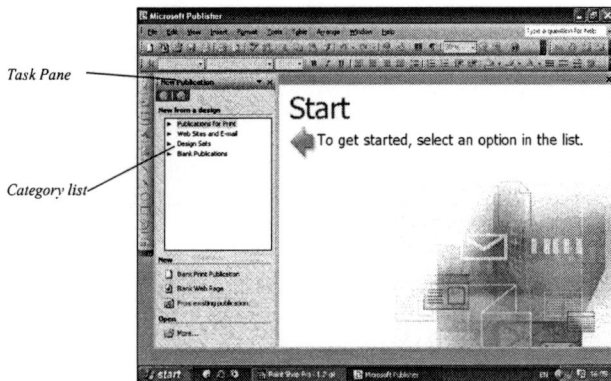

2. In the **Task Pane** drop down list, under **New from a design**, there are four options available: **Publications for Print**, **Web Sites and E-mail**, **Design Sets**, and **Blank Publications**. Select each of them from the drop down list to view their options before returning to **Publications for Print**.

3. The list below **New from a design** indicates the wide variety of options that *Publisher* has on offer. Scroll down and select **Flyers** to reveal further options within this category. The band at the top of the pictures changes to **Informational Flyers** and the templates are displayed. The one selected (has a box around it) is currently **Accent Box Informational Flyer**.

4. Select **Sale** from the list below **Flyers**.

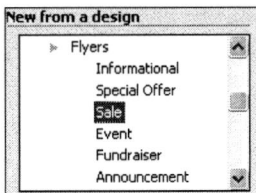

continued over

Exercise 2 - Continued

5.   The display scrolls to show the **Sale** flyer templates. The first sale flyer template, **2 Picture Product Flyer** is selected.

6.   Make further selections from the list, so that you become familiar with the kind of publications that are available.

7.   Select **Quick Publications**, the first item in the list.

8.   Click on the down arrow at the bottom of the scroll bar at the right of the screen to view further options. Once the **Butterfly Quick Publication** comes into view, click on it to select it.

*Note: The very first time Publisher is used, there will be a prompt to enter some personal details before the **Quick Publication Options** are displayed.*

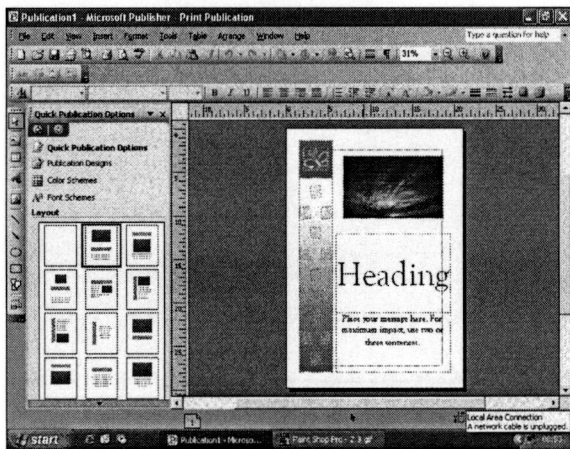

9.   The first screen shows a list of **Quick Publication Options**. The publication preview is shown on the right, although it obviously needs some editing.

10.   Click on **Color Schemes**.

*Note: It is possible for the **Quick Publication Options** to be switched off. If the **Task Pane** does not appear, select **Tools | Options** from the menu, select the **User Assistance** tab and make sure the **Use a wizard for blank publications** box is checked.*

continued over

Exercise 2 - Continued

11.   A change of colour scheme is available here. This will change the colour of the graphic at the side and give associated colours for fonts, etc. Try out a few before settling on **Rain Forest**.

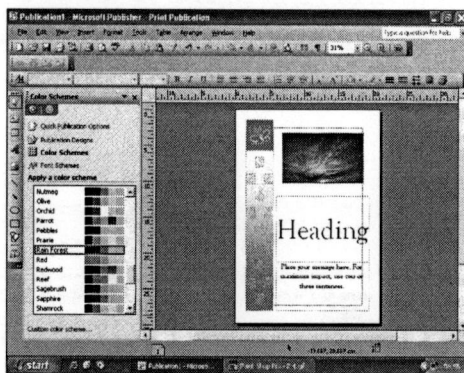

12.   Click on **Quick Publication Options**. This screen gives layout options. This affects where the text and the picture are located on the page, if at all. Try out a few before settling on **Large picture in the middle**.

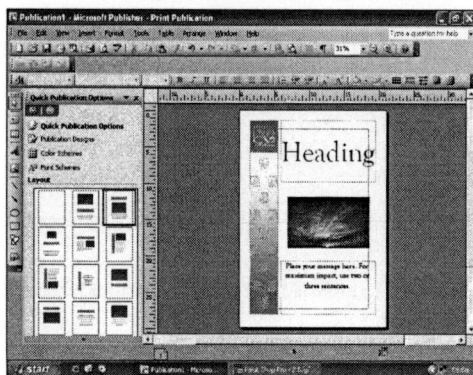

13.   To remove the **Quick Publication Options**, click the **Close** button, ☒, located at the top of the **Task Pane**.

14.   The publication is now on the full screen. Obviously, you would need to edit the text and possibly, change the picture. These skills will be learned in future exercises. For now, leave the publication on screen and move to the next exercise.

Exercise 3 - Closing a Publication

Guidelines:

A publication can be closed at any time. If the publication has not been previously saved, or if it has been modified in any way, a prompt to save it will appear. You can have more than one publication open at the same time.

Actions:

1. When certain options are selected in *Publisher 2003* the program tries to download content from **Office Online**, by connecting to the Internet. This can become annoying, especially for users without an Internet connection, or with a slow, dial up connection. While working through this guide, disable the option. Select **Tools | Options**, make sure the **General** tab is selected and click **Service Options**. A new window will appear; select **Online Content** from the list on the left.

2. If the **Show content and links from Microsoft Office Online** box is checked, uncheck it and click **OK**. If it is not checked, just click OK. Click **OK** again to close the **Options** dialog box. This change will not take effect until *Publisher* is restarted in a later exercise.

3. The publication created using the **New Publication Task Pane** should still be on screen. From the menu, select **File | Close**.

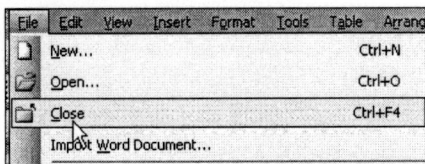

File	Edit	View	Insert	Format	Tools	Table	Arrang
New...							Ctrl+N
Open...							Ctrl+O
Close							Ctrl+F4
Import Word Document...							

4. A dialog box is displayed asking if you need to save the publication. Click **No**.

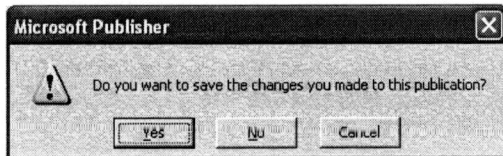

Microsoft Publisher

⚠ Do you want to save the changes you made to this publication?

[Yes]   [No]   [Cancel]

Note: *If you selected **Yes**, the **Save As** box would be displayed, allowing you to name the publication and save it for later use. **Cancel** returns to the publication without closing or saving.*

5. Notice how *Publisher* is now ready for another publication to be started.

Publisher 2003 **New CLAIT**

Exercise 4 - Creating a Blank Publication

Guidelines:

Once *Publisher* has been used the **New Publication Task Pane** is not necessarily displayed. If a blank publication is on screen as in the previous exercise then it is ready for use.

If however, there is no publication on screen then the **Task Pane** can be viewed again.

Actions:

1. The **New Publication Task Pane** should be redisplayed. If not, from the menu, select **File | New**.

2. Select **Blank Publications** from the drop down list below **New from a design**. This displays a list of the different types of blank publication available.

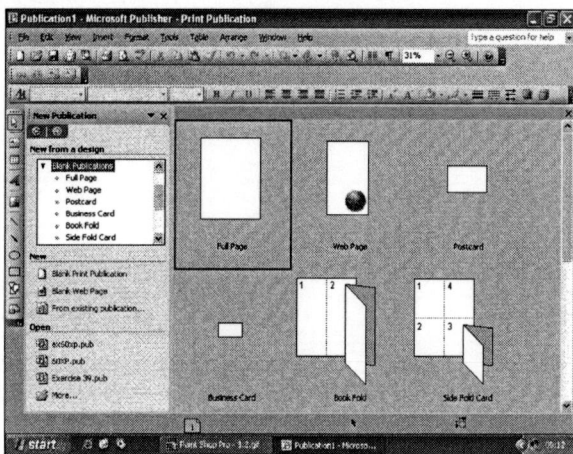

3. A blank **Full Page** is selected by default. Click on different publications from the list on the **Task Pane** to see the other options.

4. Select **Full Page** by clicking on it twice. The blank, single page publication is created, ready for editing.

*Note: If a prompt to save your work appears in these early exercises, select **No**.*

5. The **Publication Designs Task Pane** is displayed at the left of the screen. Click the **Close** button, [X]. As it will not be used on a regular basis in this guide, it is assumed that you will close the **Task Pane** where necessary.

Exercise 5 - The Publisher Screen

Guidelines:

After a publication has been selected from the **New Publication Task Pane**, the *Publisher* screen appears, displaying the page to be edited.

Actions:

1. Notice the blue **Title Bar** at the top of the screen. This shows the name of the current publication (**Publication1**), the name of the application (**Microsoft Publisher**) and the type of publication (**Print Publication**).

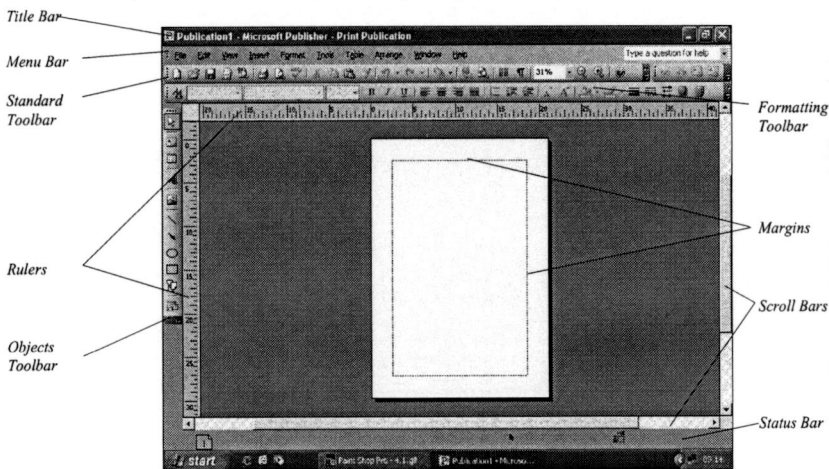

Title Bar

Menu Bar

Standard Toolbar

Formatting Toolbar

Margins

Rulers

Scroll Bars

Objects Toolbar

Status Bar

2. Look below the **Title Bar** to see the **Menu Bar**. All of the commands necessary to use *Publisher* are contained within these menus. Observe the **Standard Toolbar** beneath the **Menu Bar**, which is made up of small buttons (or tools) to perform common tasks more quickly.

3. Look at the buttons on the **Formatting Toolbar**. They are ghosted (pale and not available for selection) because the publication is empty at the moment but, at the left of the screen, is the **Objects Toolbar** where more tools are available. These tools are used to create various objects on the page.

4. The **Status Bar** at the bottom of the screen shows the number of pages in the publication and the **Object Position** and **Size** boxes. Place the cursor anywhere on the page to see its position in the **Object Position** box.

Exercise 6 - Text Boxes and Entering Text

Guidelines:

All text in a publication is contained in a **Text Box**. The box restricts the area in which the text can be viewed, but there is no limit to the number of boxes that can appear on a page. A box can be very small, or it can fill the page.

Actions:

1. From the **Objects Toolbar**, click the **Text Box Tool,** 🔲.

2. Notice how the cursor changes to a cross when you move into the publication document.

3. Click and drag a large square in the centre of the page. The **Text Box** appears on the page, with the cursor flashing inside it, ready for text to be entered.

4. Notice that the box has small white circles, known as "handles" around it. This shows that it is selected - text can only be entered into a box that is selected.

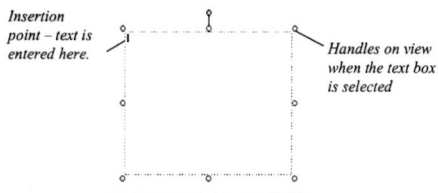

Insertion point – text is entered here.

Handles on view when the text box is selected

5. Type in the following text as accurately as possible, but do not worry if you make mistakes:

   By the time I have completed this open learning guide, I should have mastered the skills necessary to produce impressive desktop publications. I may never need to buy a birthday card again!

Note: *At this point a message in a yellow speech bubble may appear, because the text will be very small. These messages (**tippages**) appear from time to time.*

Note: *Don't worry if your text box was too small to accommodate the text. You will be increasing the size of boxes later.*

6. Press **<F9>** to zoom in to be able to read the text.

7. Leave the publication open for the next exercise.

Exercise 7 - Zoom

Guidelines:

> When text is entered into a box, it is so small that it is very difficult to read. To tackle this problem, use the **Zoom** function.

Actions:

1. There are several ways to zoom in to and out of a page. The **<F9>** key has already been used, use it now to zoom in to the page, if you haven't already zoomed in.

2. Press **<F9>** again to zoom out.

3. With the text box selected, i.e. the handles on view, select **View | Zoom**, then **Selected Objects** to zoom in again.

4. Select **View | Zoom | Whole Page** to zoom out again.

5. It is also possible to zoom in at different percentages of magnification using the menu, but there is a quicker way. Click the **Zoom In** button, , on the **Standard Toolbar** to zoom to **50%** (shown in the **Zoom Box** to the left of the).

6. Click again to zoom to **66%**. Each click of the button zooms in by the next percentage increment shown in the menu options.

7. Zoom out using the **Zoom Out** button, .

8. The **Zoom** box, , on the **Standard Toolbar** can also be used. Click on the drop down arrow at the right of the box and select **10%** from the list.

9. Use the box to zoom in to **400%**.

10. Use any method to zoom to **Whole Page**.

11. Leave the publication open for the next exercise.

Note: *Words with jagged red lines below are spelling errors or words that Publisher does not recognise, such as names.*

Exercise 8 - Closing Publisher

Guidelines:

> Publisher can be closed at any time.

Note: When closing Publisher, if the current publication has not been saved, a warning will be displayed asking if it is to be saved.

Actions:

1. Click on the **File** menu.

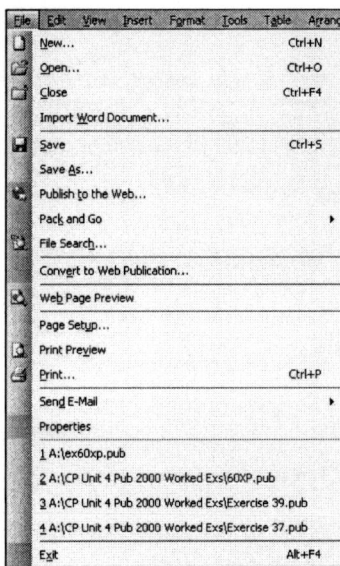

File	Edit	View	Insert	Format	Tools	Table	Arrang

```
New...                                    Ctrl+N
Open...                                   Ctrl+O
Close                                     Ctrl+F4
Import Word Document...
Save                                      Ctrl+S
Save As...
Publish to the Web...
Pack and Go                               ▶
File Search...
Convert to Web Publication...
Web Page Preview
Page Setup...
Print Preview
Print...                                  Ctrl+P
Send E-Mail                               ▶
Properties
1 A:\ex60xp.pub
2 A:\CP Unit 4 Pub 2000 Worked Exs\60XP.pub
3 A:\CP Unit 4 Pub 2000 Worked Exs\Exercise 39.pub
4 A:\CP Unit 4 Pub 2000 Worked Exs\Exercise 37.pub
Exit                                      Alt+F4
```

2. Place the mouse pointer over **Exit** and click once. The following message appears:

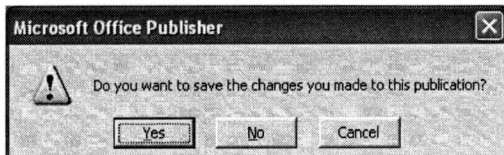

```
Microsoft Office Publisher                          [X]

   ⚠   Do you want to save the changes you made to this publication?

            [ Yes ]      No          Cancel
```

3. Click **No** to close *Publisher* without saving the publication.

Exercise 9 - Revision

1. Start *Publisher*.

2. Use the **New Publication Task Pane** to create a **Wallet Sized Calendar** of any type.

3. Close this publication without saving.

4. Open a blank, full page publication from the **New Publication Task Pane**. Close the **Task Pane**.

5. Draw a large **Text Box** on the page.

6. Enter the following text, zooming in to read it:

   When it was opened in 1889, the Eiffel Tower was the tallest manmade structure in the world. Designed by a bridge builder, the tower is composed of iron girders held together by bolts, like a giant Meccano set. The feet of the tower are hydraulic, so that it can move slightly in high winds. Due to suicide attempts (many of which were successful) barriers have been erected to prevent visitors climbing over the edge.

7. Close the publication <u>without</u> saving.

Exercise 10 - Revision

1. Open a blank publication, if there is not one available on screen.

2. Draw a text box in the middle of the page.

3. Zoom in to **66%**.

4. Enter the following text:

   You are free to use the clip art in Publisher for any use, except that you may not resell or redistribute the clip art for value in any library or clip art product consisting primarily of clip art images.

5. On the same page, draw another text box.

6. Zoom in to **75%**.

7. Enter your name in this box.

8. Close the publication <u>without</u> saving.

Exercise 11 - Revision

1. On a blank publication, draw a small text box near the top margin.

2. Enter your name.

3. Draw another text box beneath the first and enter the name of a friend.

4. Draw as many boxes as required to enter all of your friends' names.

5. Close the publication without saving.

Exercise 12 - Revision

1. **Exit** *Publisher.*

2. Open *Publisher* again.

3. Use the **New Publication Task Pane** to create a **Take Out Menu**. Look first under **Menus**.

4. Use the **Crisscross Design**.

5. Change the **Colour Scheme** to **Sunset**.

6. Close the publication without saving.

7. **Exit** *Publisher.*

Section 2

Publications

By the end of this Section you should be able to:

Save and Open Publications
Move the Cursor around a Publication
Select and Edit Text
Change Page Setup
Print a Composite Proof

Exercise 13 - Saving a Publication

Guidelines:

A publication must be saved if it is to be used again. There are two main ways to save a publication, depending on whether it is a newly created publication, or whether it has previously been saved and given a name.

Actions:

1. Start *Publisher* and create a new, blank publication.

2. Draw a **Text Box** anywhere on the page. Enter a couple of sentences about yourself and your hobbies.

3. Select the **File** menu and choose the **Save As** command. The **Save As** dialog box will then appear.

4. Use the drop down list from the **Save in** box to locate the area where your publications are to be saved. Consult your tutor if you are not sure.

Places Bar

5. The publication must be given a name. Enter **Personal** in the **File name** box.

Note: A filename can be of any length. Choose a meaningful name but do not use any of the following characters: ><"*?:\ /;|

6. Click the **Save** button, [Save], at the bottom right of the dialog box.

7. Select **File | Close** to clear the screen.

*Note: A previously named publication can be saved to the same location under the same name by clicking the **Save** button, on the **Toolbar**. When a new document is to be saved, selecting **Save** will display the **Save As** dialog box.*

Exercise 14 - Opening a Publication

Guidelines:

Once a publication has been created and saved, it can be opened at any time.

Actions:

1. Before starting this exercise, check that you know the location of the data files for **Unit 6**.

2. The text area of the screen should be clear from the end of the previous exercise. Select **File | Open** to display the **Open Publication** dialog box.

*Note: The **Open Publication** dialog box can be displayed by clicking the **Open** button, , on the **Standard Toolbar**. To start a new, blank publication, click the **New** button, .*

3. From the **Look in** box, select the location where the data files are saved, and select **Preview** from the drop-down list of the **Views** button.

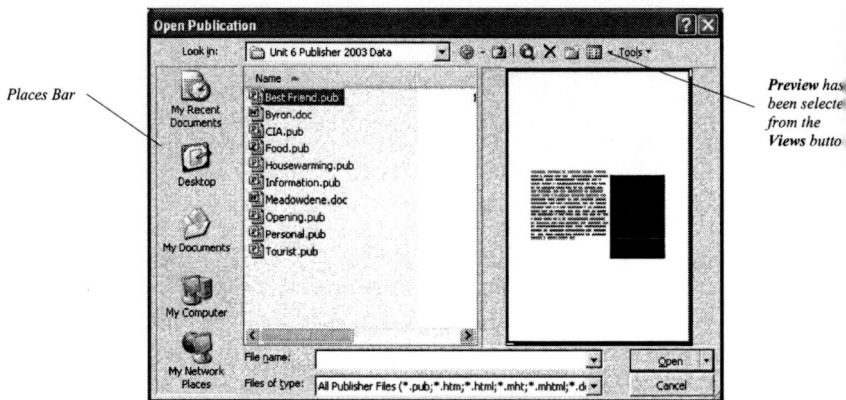

Places Bar

Preview has been selected from the Views butto

4. Select the file **Best Friend** and then click the **Open** button.

5. Use **File | Close** to close the publication, then select **File** from the **Menu Bar**. The last four publications that have been used are listed at the bottom.

6. Click once on the file name ending in **Personal** to open the file, then select **File | Close** to close it.

Exercise 15 - Cursor Movement

Guidelines:

The quickest way to move the cursor around a text box is to position the mouse and click the left button, but there are also some useful key movements.

Actions:

1. Open the publication **CIA**. Select the text box and zoom in to see the text.

2. Click in the middle of the second line of text, starting **Founded in1985....**

3. Press **<End>**. The cursor is now flashing at the end of the line.

4. Press **<Home>**. Now the cursor is at the beginning of the line.

5. Press **<Ctrl End>** to move to the end of the text.

6. Press **<Ctrl Home>** to move to the start of the text.

7. Place the cursor in the middle of the second paragraph.

8. The cursor keys, ↑, ←, → and ↓, can also be used to move around text. Press each key in turn to move around.

9. These keys can also be used with the **<Ctrl>** key. Press **<Ctrl →>** to move to the next word.

10. Move back one word by pressing **<Ctrl ←>**.

11. Use the key press **<Ctrl ↓>** to move down to the start of the next paragraph.

12. Press **<Ctrl ↑>** to move to the previous paragraph.

13. Leave the publication open for the next exercise.

Exercise 16 - Selecting Text

Guidelines:

It is important to be familiar with the different selection methods because text has to be selected before it can be edited or formatted.

Actions:

1. The publication **CIA** should still be open from the previous exercise. If not, open it.

2. Text can be selected by clicking the mouse where the selection is to begin, then dragging the mouse with the button still held down over the area to be selected. When the mouse button is released, the text will be highlighted, showing it has been selected. Select the word **specialist** from the second line of text in the text box by clicking and dragging the mouse across it.

3. Click the mouse once. The text has now been deselected.

4. A quick way to select a word is to move the mouse pointer over the word (it will look like a letter **I** when over the text) and double click. Select the last word in the box by double clicking.

Note: A paragraph can be selected by clicking the mouse three times, anywhere within the paragraph.

5. The key press **<Ctrl A>** will select a full box of text. Select the text this way.

6. Close the publication. Do <u>not</u> save any changes if prompted.

Exercise 17 - Editing Text

Guidelines:

It is often necessary to change text after it has been entered, because of errors or omissions.

Actions:

1. Open the publication **Information** and zoom in to read the text.

2. Text is entered where the cursor is flashing (the **Insertion Point**). Move to the end of the text and press the **<Spacebar>** to create a space.

3. Type in the following sentence: **There are also "Pint Questions", where the correct answer wins a pint of guest ale.**

4. In the first article, third paragraph, change **...beam of green light...** to **...beam of violet light....** Select **green**, then type the replacement text. The highlighted text is replaced.

5. The **<Delete>** key can be used to delete single characters to the right of the cursor. Position the cursor in the last sentence of the same article, before **made** and keep pressing **<Delete>** until the word and full stop have been deleted.

6. The **<Backspace>** key, usually a left pointing arrow above **<Enter>**, deletes text to the left of the cursor. Delete the rest of the sentence using the **<Backspace>** key.

7. Save the publication as **Information1** and close it.

Exercise 18 - Page Setup

Guidelines:

Page Setup governs how a publication is printed. The **Publication Layout** for example, can be changed - whether it is printed normally, or like a greeting card.

Orientation – whether it prints in **Portrait**, ⌐, or **Landscape**, ⌐, can also be changed.

Paper Size is changed via **File | Page Setup**. The **Paper Size** drop down list has the most common sizes. As you will only use the default size of A4, changing paper size will not be practised here.

Actions:

1. Open the publication **Best Friend**.

2. Select **File | Page Setup** to display the following dialog box.

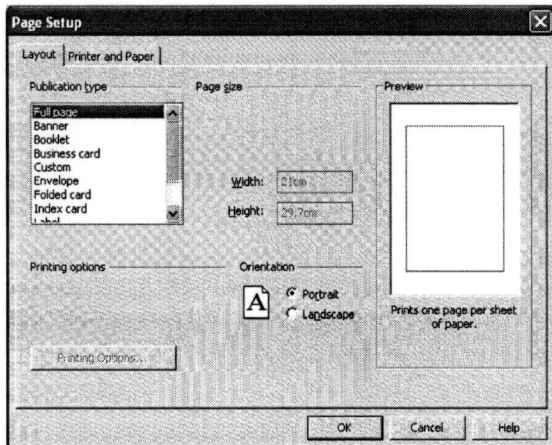

3. Select the **Business card** option from the drop down list below **Publication type** and notice the changes to the layout that appear in the dialog box.

4. Reselect **Full page**.

5. Change the **Orientation** to **Landscape**. Notice how the **Preview** changes to reflect the selection. Click **Cancel**.

6. Leave the publication open for the next exercise.

Exercise 19 - Setting Margins and Layout Guides

Guidelines:

Margin and Layout Guides help to line up objects on the page. The blue dotted lines around the page of every publication are the guides, but more can be added to make the positioning more precise. Layout Guides are not printed. While margins can be set on the page, text and picture frames can be placed outside them. You must, therefore, be careful when placing boxes making sure they will appear within the printed area for your particular printer.

Note: ***Baseline Guides****, available from the same dialog box as the other guides, can also be used to help align lines of text, but they are not used in this course.*

Actions:

1. Using the publication **Best Friend**, select **Arrange | Layout Guides** to display the **Layout Guides** dialog box.

2. Normally, the only guides showing are the **Margin Guides** around the edge of the page. These can be altered, but remember that boxes or frames may overlap them.

3. Select the **Left Margin Guide** value. Type in **5**.

4. For the **Right Margin Guide**, click on the up arrow and change the value to **4.5**.

5. Change the **Top Margin Guide** by clicking and dragging across the value to select it and typing in **8**.

continued over

　　　　　　　© CiA Training Ltd 2004

Exercise 19 - Continued

6. Click **OK**. Notice how the boxes already placed on the page are unaffected, but the **Margin Guides** have changed to the values entered.

7. A grid can be created on the page to help line up objects. Select **Arrange | Layout Guides** again.

8. Select the **Grid Guides** tab and change the number of **Columns** to **4** using the up arrow at the right of the **Columns** box.

9. Change the number of **Rows** to **6**. Notice how the **Preview** changes.

10. Click **OK**.

11. Select **Arrange | Layout Guides** and the **Grid Guides** tab.

12. Change the number of **Columns** to **2** and the number of **Rows** to **4**. Click **OK**.

13. Close the publication without saving.

Exercise 20 - Printing

Guidelines:

A print out from a publication can take many forms. However, you will only need to print out a "composite proof". This means that all items on the page will be printed on one page.

This is as opposed to a "colour separation proof" that will print only one colour per page. So if you had a publication with blue text and picture colours of blue and red, then there would have to be two proofs produced, one for the blue and one for the red.

If the **Print** button, , is used, a single copy of the entire publication is printed.

continued over

Exercise 20 - Continued

Actions:

1. Open the publication **Best Friend**.

2. Change the orientation to **Landscape**.

3. Select **File | Print** to display the **Print** dialog box.

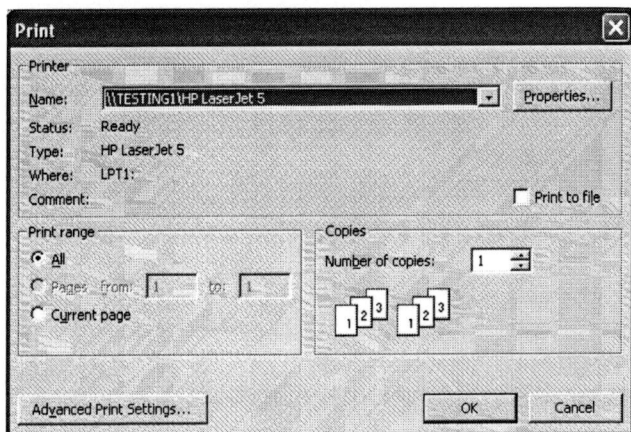

4. The **Print range** option is automatically set to **All**. This means that the whole publication will be printed. In this case, there is only one page, so it is all right to leave the option as it is. The **Number of copies** option is automatically set to **1** (if you want to print more than one copy, use the arrows at the right to change the number, or type directly into the box). Click **OK** to print the publication.

5. Save the publication as **Orientation** and close it.

6. Open **Tourist**.

7. Click the **Print** button, 🖨, to print one copy of the publication.

8. Close it <u>without</u> saving.

Exercise 21 - Revision

1. On a blank publication, draw a text box and enter the following text:

   Welcome to the first edition of Meadowdene Today, our local community newsletter, to be published weekly. The editor would appreciate interesting editorial contributions from any members of the community.

2. Change **Meadowdene Today** to **Meadowdene Weekly**.

3. Delete **, to be published weekly**.

4. Delete **editorial**.

5. Draw a second, small text box in the bottom left corner and enter your own name.

6. Print a single copy of the publication.

7. Save it as **Weekly** and close it.

Exercise 22 - Revision

1. Open the publication **CIA**.

2. Select the text, **Founded in 1985,** found under the title and delete it.

3. There are two occurrences of **10 years**. Change both of these to **15 years**.

4. At the end of the text, press **<Enter>**.

5. Enter the following text:

   New CLAIT for Office 2003 is the latest, exciting range from CiA Training Ltd. It incorporates many self-teach units, that work towards the New CLAIT qualification.

6. Print a copy of the publication.

7. Close it <u>without</u> saving.

Exercise 23 - Revision

1. Open the publication **Best Friend**.
2. Change the orientation of the page to **Landscape**.
3. Insert a text box at the top left corner and add your name.
4. Print a copy.
5. Save the publication as **Long Dog** and close it.

Exercise 24 - Revision

1. Open the publication **Opening**.
2. Select the text **20th December** and replace it with **15th July**.
3. Use a key press to move to the end of the box.
4. Delete the number **3** and type in **4**.
5. Replace the word **Giovanni's** with your name, remembering to replace the **'s**.
6. Print a copy.
7. Close the publication <u>without</u> saving.

Exercise 25 - Revision

1. On a blank publication, change the margins to **5cms** all round.
2. Draw a text box that exactly fits these new margins.
3. Close the publication <u>without</u> saving.

Section 3

Text Formatting

By the end of this Section you should be able to:

Change Text Fonts, Size and Colour

Change Alignment

Change Paragraph Spacing

Apply First Line Indent

Exercise 26 - Changing Fonts and Text Size

Guidelines:

A font is a type or style of print. There are two different types of font: **serif** and **sans serif**. A serif font, e.g. Times New Roman, Book Antiqua, has extra lines or curls on the 'stalk' of the letters (**q**); a sans serif font, e.g. Arial, Comic Sans MS, Tahoma, does not (**q**). A combination of the software in use and the selected printer determines which fonts are available for use.

Note: If any of the fonts used in the following exercises are not available, select a different one.

The size of text can also be changed to improve the look of a publication – many different text sizes can be used within the same publication. Size is measured in **points**: the larger the point size, the larger the text. When a text box is created, the point size will automatically be set at **10**.

Actions:

1. Open the publication **Food** and zoom in to read the text.

2. This menu needs to be much more eye-catching - applying different fonts will help. Select the first line, **Chez Pascale**.

3. Click on the drop down arrow at the right of the **Font** box, Times New Roman ▾ on the **Formatting Toolbar**, scroll up the list (which displays a preview of how the font will look) and select **Forte** – a serif font.

*Note: The font and size can also be changed by selecting **Format | Font** and selecting options before clicking **OK**. Once a font has been used, it is shown at the top of the **Font** drop down list.*

4. Select the following words and apply the same font: **Menu, Entrées, Main Meals** and **Desserts**.

5. Select the remaining text and change the font to **French Script MT** – a serif font.

6. This text is now very small. Select all of the text and click the **Increase Font Size** button, [A] on the **Formatting Toolbar**, three times.

*Note: The **Decrease Font Size** button, [A], can be used in the same way to reduce text size.*

7. Select **Chez Pascale**, then click the drop down arrow at the right of the **Size** box, 14 ▾ and select **16** to increase the size.

8. Save the publication as **Food2** and close it.

Exercise 27 - Alignment

Guidelines:

Alignment refers to how text appears on the screen in relation to the margins of the text box. Text can be aligned in four ways: to the **Left**, **Right**, **Centre** or **Justified** (straight left and right margins). Many people prefer to justify text, because of its neat appearance, while **Centre** alignment can be used for flyers, menus, etc.

Actions:

1. Open the publication **Tourist** and click in the text frame to select it. The text is aligned to the **Left**. The **Formatting Toolbar** becomes active when a text frame is selected. Alignment is changed using these buttons on the **Formatting Toolbar**:

    Align Left

    Centre

    Align Right

    Justify

Note: If all of the alignment buttons are not displayed, click the chevrons, at the end of the **Formatting** toolbar to reveal the hidden ones.

2. Click in the first paragraph, then click the **Align Right** button, See how the paragraph has changed.

Note: It is not necessary to select a whole paragraph before changing its alignment. Just click once anywhere within the paragraph to be aligned, before selecting one of the buttons.

3. Centre the last paragraph by clicking within the paragraph, then selecting the **Center** button,

4. Click in the first paragraph and change its alignment by selecting the **Justify** button,

5. Select all of the text. Click to centre the document.

6. Create a text box at the top of the publication and enter your name. Centre the text, change the font to any serif font and change the size to **18pt**.

7. Print the publication and close it without saving.

continued over

Exercise 27 - Continued

8.   Open the publication **Food2**, saved in Exercise 26.

9.   Select all of the text.

10.   Centre align the selected text.

11.   Save the publication using the same name.

12.   Close the publication.

Exercise 28 - Paragraph Formatting

Guidelines:

Paragraphs can have spacing applied before or after them to make the text easier to read. It is also a recognised convention that, occasionally, the first line of a paragraph is indented, i.e. the first line is further from the left edge of the text box than the remainder of the paragraph.

Actions:

1.   Open the publication **CIA** and zoom in on the text box to read the text.

2.   The text is not easy to read because there is no spacing between the paragraphs. Select all of the text in the text box.

3.   From the **Menu Bar**, select **Format | Paragraph**.

4.   Select to have a **12pt** space **After** each paragraph – use the **up** spinner arrow, to alter the value or click and drag across the original value and type in the new one.

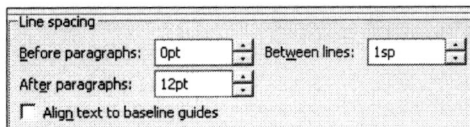

Line spacing			
Before paragraphs:	0pt	Between lines:	1sp
After paragraphs:	12pt		
☐ Align text to baseline guides			

5.   Click **OK** to apply the change.

6.   Place the cursor in the first paragraph.

7.   Display the **Paragraph** dialog box again and change the **After** value to **20pt** for this paragraph only.

continued over

Exercise 28 - Continued

8. With the cursor in the same paragraph, select **Format | Paragraph** again.

9. Drop down the list from the **Preset Indentation** area and select **1st Line Indent**.

Indentation			
_P_reset:	1st Line Indent ▼	_L_eft:	0cm
_F_irst line:	1cm	_R_ight:	0cm

10. Click **OK** to apply the indent.

11. With the cursor in the same paragraph, open the **Paragraph** dialog box again.

12. Drop down the **Alignment** list and select **Justified**. It is always useful to know that should more than one type of formatting to be applied, it can be done from one dialog box.

13. Click **OK**.

14. Print the publication and close it <u>without</u> saving.

Exercise 29 - Revision

1.   Open the publication **Information1** which was saved in Exercise 17.

2.   Select all of the text in the box. Change the font size to **14pt**.

3.   Zoom in to **75%**.

4.   The text is made up of a series of newspaper articles. Select each article title in turn and change the font to **Colonna MT** and the size to **20pt**.

5.   Change the font and size of the text in the first article to **Arial 12pt**.

6.   Change the font and size of the text in the second article to **Elephant 11pt**.

7.   Save the changes and close the publication.

Exercise 30 - Revision

1.   Open the publication **CIA**.

2.   Select all of the text and fully justify it.

3.   Click in the first paragraph. Change the paragraph spacing **after** to **10pt**.

4.   Select the remainder of the paragraphs. Change the paragraph spacing **after** these paragraphs to **14pt**.

5.   At the end of the text, press **<Enter>** and type in your name.

6.   Print a copy and close the publication without saving.

Exercise 31 - Revision

1.   Open the publication **Information1**.

2.   Select all of the text and change the paragraph spacing **after** to **3pt**.

3.   Indent the first line of each article.

4.   Add your name at the end of the text and print a copy.

5.   Save the changes and close the publication.

Section 4

Working with Boxes

By the end of this Section you should be able to:

Change Text Box Properties
Move/Resize a Box
Apply Borders
Import Text Files
Use Columns

Exercise 32 - Text Box Properties

Guidelines:

Text box margins can be changed within the **Format Text Box** dialog box. Columns can also be added from here.

Actions:

1. Open the publication **CIA** and select the text box.

2. Zoom in to read the text and select **Format | Text Box**.

3. Select the **Text Box** tab, this allows the margins to be modified.

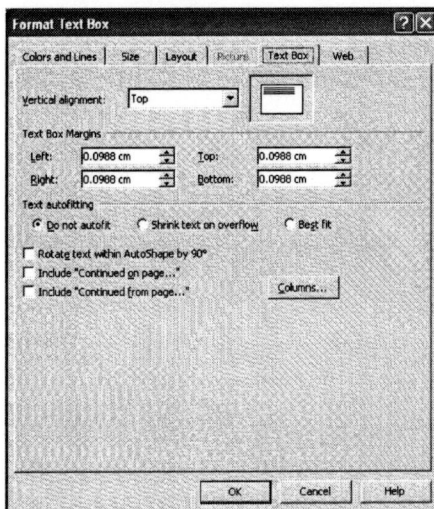

4. To increase the space between the edge of the text box and the text, click in the **Left** margin box and type **0.75cm**.

5. Move to the **Right** margin box and enter **0.75cm**.

6. In the same way, change the **Top** and **Bottom** margins to **0.75cm**. Click **OK**.

7. Redisplay the **Text Box** dialog box.

8. Change all of the margins to **0.2cm**.

9. Save the publication as **CIA2** and close it.

Exercise 33 - Moving and Resizing Boxes

Guidelines:

A text box can be moved to any position on a page, but it must first be selected (have its handles visible). A box is moved by positioning the mouse over an edge, not a handle, and clicking and dragging. To change the size of a box, the mouse must be moved over a handle before clicking and dragging.

Actions:

1. Open the publication **Best Friend** and select the text box beside the picture.

2. Don't zoom in, as the whole page should be in view.

3. To move the box, move the mouse over any edge of the box until a **Helpful Pointer**, ⊕ appears.

Note: These pointers can be switched off. If they are not visible, select **Tools | Options** and the **User Assistance** tab. Check **Use helpful mouse pointers** and click **OK**.

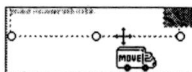

4. Click and drag the box down to the bottom left corner of the page, then release the mouse.

5. Now move the mouse over the top right handle of the box until another **Helpful Pointer**, ᴿᴱˢᴵᶻᴱ , appears.

continued over

Exercise 33 - Continued

6.   Click and drag upwards and to the right until the box fills most of the page.

7.   Move the mouse over the middle handle at the top of the box until **RESIZE** appears and reduce the size of the box to about half a page.

Note: *Notice how the text is always wrapped around the picture.*

8.   Use the top right corner handle to reduce the size of the box to a quarter of a page.

Note: *If at any time ⊞••• appears at the base of the text box, as below, it has been made too small to accommodate the text. If necessary, increase the size of the box using a handle until ⊞••• disappears.*

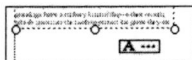

9.   Now move the box to the middle of the page.

10.   Leave the publication open.

Exercise 34 - Using Best Fit

Guidelines:

Sometimes, text needs to fit across the width of a box exactly. However, if the size of the box has not yet been finally decided, then *Publisher* has a tool that can help.

Actions:

1. The **Best Friend** publication should still be open from the previous exercise. If not, open it.

2. Draw a text box at the top of the page from margin to margin.

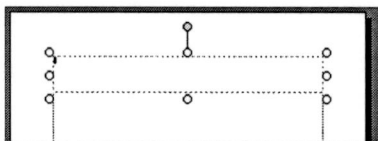

3. Enter the text **My Best Friend** and select it.

4. **Centre** the text. It does not matter at this point that the text is small.

5. From the menu select **Format | AutoFit Text**. From the further options select **Best Fit**.

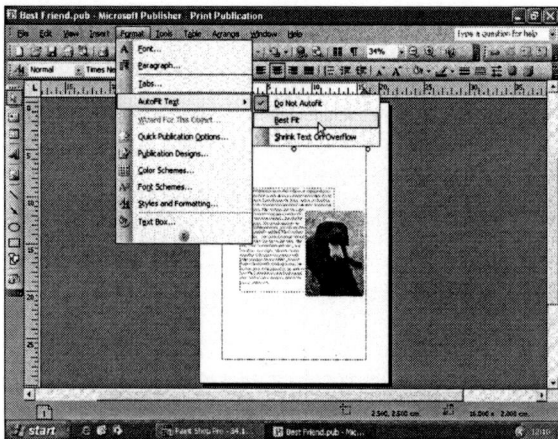

continued over

Exercise 34 - Continued

6.   The text immediately fills the box.

7.   The test, of course, is what happens when the box size changes. Select the middle handle at the right of the box and drag it to the left. This makes the box smaller. The text resizes itself accordingly.

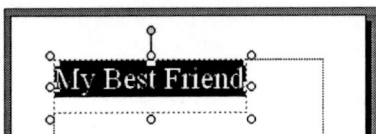

8.   Try resizing the box in other directions to test **Best Fit**.

9.   Save the publication as **Best Friend1** and close it.

10.   Open the publication **CIA2**, saved in Exercise 32.

11.   Draw a text box at the bottom of the page from margin to margin.

12.   Enter the text **CiA Training Ltd**.

13.   Select all of the text in this box make it **Best Fit** the box.

14.   Centre the text.

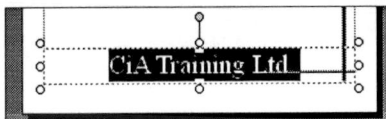

15.   Resize the box so that it is not as tall. The text becomes smaller accordingly. .

16.   Save the changes and close the publication.

Exercise 35 - Applying Borders and Lines

Guidelines:

A border can be added to a box to make it stand out from the rest of the page. Lines can also be used to separate parts of the publication. They can also be added between columns of text, although this will be covered later.

Actions:

1. Open the publication **Information1**.

2. Select the text box and zoom in to see it more clearly.

3. Click the **Line/Border Style** button, , on the **Formatting** toolbar. A drop down menu appears.

4. Select **More Lines** to display the **Format Text Box** dialog box.

5. Border colour can be changed from this dialog box. Below **Line**, click the **Color** drop down list, then select **More Colors**.

continued over

Exercise 35 - Continued

6.   Select **Purple**.

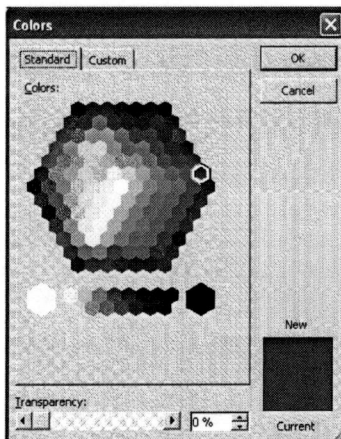

7.   Click **OK** and then click **OK** again to close the dialog box.

8.   Click the **Line/Border Style** button again, select **More Lines**

9.   Use the **up** spinner arrow beside the **Weight** button to increase the line weight to **2pt**. Click **OK** to apply the border.

10.   You have already used the **Objects** toolbar several times to add text boxes. Notice that there are several more tools available. The **Drawing** tools allow lines, boxes, circles and ellipses to be drawn on a publication, along with various other shapes. For the time being you will only use lines.

11.   Select the **Line Tool**, . The cursor changes to a cross.

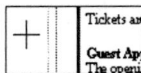

12.   Place the cross where the line is to start, on the box edge above **Guest Appearance**, and drag across to the finishing point, the opposite box edge. Make sure the line is straight.

Note: Hold down the <Shift> key while dragging to draw a straight line.

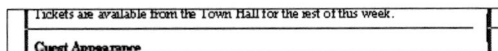

13.   Once the mouse button is released the line is drawn.

14.   Leave the publication open for the next exercise.

Exercise 36 - Line Formatting

Guidelines:

Once a line has been drawn it can be formatted in various ways. These rules apply to all drawn objects.

Actions:

1. The **Information1** publication should still be open from the previous exercise, if not, open it now.

2. Select the line that has just been drawn – a line is selected when the handles are on view at each end. Line length can be altered by clicking and dragging one of the handles.

3. Click the drop down arrow on the **Line Color** button, 🖊, on the **Formatting Toolbar**. Select a blue colour from those available. The line changes to blue.

4. Click the **Line/Border Style** button, ☰ and select the widest line available.

5. Click **Line/Border Style** again and select **More Lines**.

6. The **Format AutoShape** dialog box is displayed. All formatting can be changed here.

7. Click on **Dashed**, and select **Round Dot**.

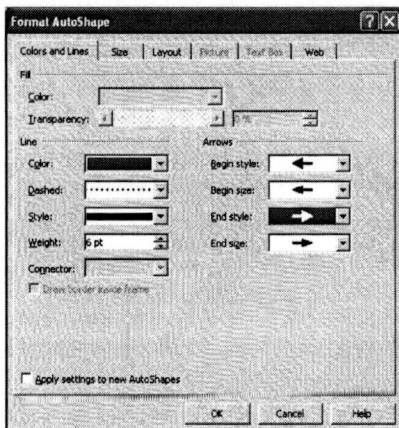

8. Select the type of arrow as shown in the diagram to the right, for both the beginning and end of the line.

9. Click **OK**.

10. Close the publication without saving.

Exercise 37 - Importing Text Files

Guidelines:

Text, which already exists in another location, can be inserted into a publication. Once a text box has been drawn, it is easy to insert a file.

Actions:

1. On a new publication, draw a large text box to cover the top two thirds of the page.

2. With the box selected, click **Insert | Text File** to display the **Insert Text** dialog box.

3. Make sure the **Look in** box shows the location where the data files are saved and that the **Files of type** box shows **All Text Formats**.

4. Click on **Byron** to select the file.

5. Click **OK**. The message **Publisher is converting this file** appears. The file is inserted in to the text box.

6. Select the text and change the font to **Book Antiqua**, then justify the text.

7. Save the publication as **Lord Byron** and close it.

Exercise 38 - Columns

Guidelines:

Columns divide the text vertically into sections within its box. This is a different way of presenting text, which would look really effective in a newsletter, for example.

Actions:

1. Open **Information**, select the box and zoom to **66%**.

2. Select **Format | Text Box** to display the **Format Text Box** dialog box.

3. Select the **Text Box** tab and then the **Columns** button, [Columns...].

4. In the **Columns** area, change the number of columns to **2**.

Columns

Columns

Number: 2

Spacing: 0.198 cm

Preview

OK   Cancel

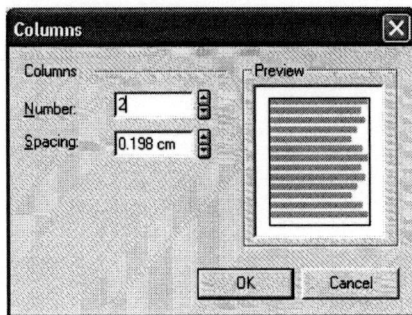

5. Click **OK** and **OK** again to divide the box into two columns.

6. Display the **Format Text Box** dialog box.

7. Increase the number of columns to **3,** click **OK** and **OK** again.

8. Print 1 copy of the publication.

9. Save the publication as **Articles** and close it.

Exercise 39 - Column Spacing

Guidelines:

> The space between columns can be altered to make reading easier. Sometimes lines are drawn between columns to further separate them.

Actions:

1. Open the publication **Lord Byron**, saved in Exercise 37. Select the text in the box and ensure that it is fully justified.

2. Select **Format | Text Box**. Select the **Text Box** tab and click the **Columns** button, `Columns...`. Make **2** columns and alter the **Spacing** below the **Columns** number to **1.2** (use the up arrow or overtype with **1.2**).

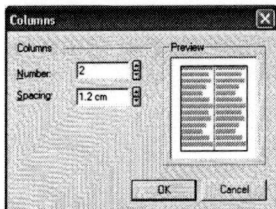

3. Click **OK** and **OK** again to apply the columns and spacing.

4. The columns are not necessarily balanced, i.e. the same length. This can easily be adjusted by changing the size of the text box. Resize the text box from the bottom using the middle handle.

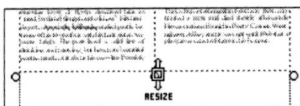

5. The resizing will have to be up or down depending on the original size of the box.

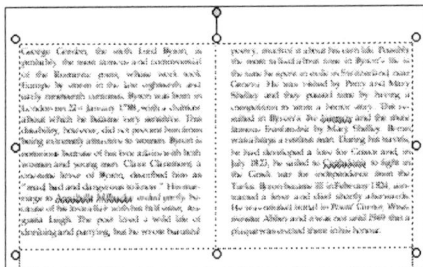

continued over

Exercise 39 - Continued

6. If there is a **Text in Overflow** button, [A···], on view at the bottom of the box, then not all of the text is in the box. Resize again until the columns are balanced.

7. It is acceptable for the columns to be balanced within **2** lines of each other as below.

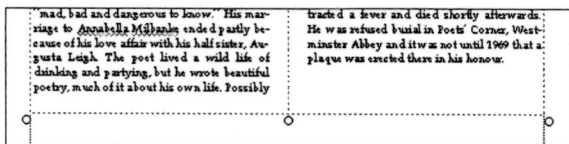

'mad, bad and dangerous to know.' His marriage to Annabella Milbanke ended partly because of his love affair with his half sister, Augusta Leigh. The poet lived a wild life of drinking and partying, but he wrote beautiful poetry, much of it about his own life. Possibly	tracked a fever and died shortly afterwards. He was refused burial in Poets' Corner, Westminster Abbey and it was not until 1969 that a plaque was erected there in his honour.

8. There is a dotted dividing line between the columns. Select the line drawing tool and draw a vertical line on this divide. The length of the line may have to be adjusted if the box is changed in any way.

9. Place the cursor at the beginning of the text and press **<Enter>**.

10. In the space left type in **Lord Byron**. Select this text and change it to **Arial Black** size **18pt**.

11. The columns are no longer balanced. Delete this text and remove the blank line.

12. Move the text box and line down to create a space above.

13. Draw a text box above the existing one so that it is the same width.

14. Type **Lord Byron** into this box. **Centre** this text and make it **Best Fit**. This is the best way to make a heading stretch across two or more columns.

15. Give this heading box a border from the **Line/Border style** button.

16. Draw a small text box at the bottom of the page.

17. Insert your name.

18. Change to a **sans serif** font with the size at **12pt**.

19. Print 1 copy of the publication

20. Save the changes and close the publication.

Exercise 40 - Revision

1. Open a blank publication.

2. Draw a large text box form margin to margin.

3. Insert the text file **Meadowdene**.

4. Resize the box so that it fits the text.

5. Close the publication <u>without</u> saving.

Exercise 41 - Revision

1. Open the publication **Information1**.

2. Select all of the text in the box.

3. Apply **Best Fit**.

4. Use a key press to go to the beginning of the text.

5. Press **<Enter>**.

6. In the space type your name and press **<Enter>** again. The text will re-adjust its size.

7. Print 1 copy of the publication.

8. Save the changes and close it.

Exercise 42 - Revision

1. Open the publication **Food**.

2. Select all of the text in the box.

3. Change the font size to **16pt** and centre all of the text.

4. Resize the sides of the box to the margins. This will ensure that the text is centred on the page.

5. Resize the bottom of the box up to the text.

6. Move the box down so that it looks central on the page.

7. Draw a small text box near the bottom of the page and enter your name.

8. Centre the text.

9. Print a copy.

10. Close the publication <u>without</u> saving.

Exercise 43 - Revision

1. Open the publication **Tourist**.

2. Select the text box.

3. Use the **Format Text Box** dialog box and the **Text Box** tab to adjust the internal margins of the box to **0.35cm**.

4. Select all of the text in the box and fully justify it.

5. Move the box to the top left corner, but stay within the margins.

6. Draw a small text box near the bottom of the page and enter your name.

7. Print a copy.

8. Close the publication <u>without</u> saving.

Exercise 44 - Revision

1. Open the publication **Food**.

2. Select all of the text and centre align it.

3. Resize the box so that it just fits the text.

4. Put a **blue 4pt** border around the box.

5. Make the text in the box **Best Fit**.

6. Resize the box so that it reaches the margins.

7. Select the text **Chez Pascale** and change the font and size to **Arial Black 36pt**.

8. Replace **Pascale** with your name.

9. Add a short **orange 1pt** line after **Entreés, Main Meals** and **Desserts**.

10. Place arrows on both ends of all of the lines.

11. Print a copy.

12. Close the publication without saving.

Note: *Check the sample publication in* **Answers** *at the end of the guide.*

Exercise 45 - Revision

1. On a blank publication, draw a large text box.

2. Insert the text file **Meadowdene**.

3. Change the font size of all of the text to **16pt**.

4. Resize the box so that it fits the text.

5. Use the **Format Text Box** dialog box to place **2** columns in this box.

6. Change the spacing between the columns to **0.95cm**.

7. Justify all of the text.

8. Move the box down the page.

9. Delete the text **History of Meadowdene** and the following blank line.

10. Resize the box so that the columns are balanced.

11. Draw a new text box above the columns and to the same width.

12. Type in **History of Meadowdene** and centre the text.

13. Make it **Best Fit**.

14. Place a ½ **pt** border around both boxes.

15. Draw a similar line between the columns.

16. Print 1 copy of the publication.

17. Save the publication as **Village** and close it.

*Note: Check the sample publication in **Answers** at the end of the guide.*

Section 5

Pictures

By the end of this Section you should be able to:

Use the Clip Gallery
Insert and Delete Pictures
Import Pictures
Move and Resize Pictures
Add Borders and Colour
Wrap Text around Pictures

Exercise 46 - The Clip Gallery

Guidelines:

Pictures can be added to a publication in two ways: either by importing a picture file, or by using the **Clip Gallery**.

The **Clip Art Task Pane** contains graphics, which are sorted into categories, so the appropriate clip can be found quickly.

Note: *There is not much **Clip Art** supplied with Office 2003, but if desired you can download graphics from **Office Online**, by connecting to the Internet, as mentioned in Exercise 3. However, this may take a long time if you have a dial up connection.*

*To enable the option, select **Tools | Options**, make sure the **General** tab is selected and click **Service Options**. A new window will appear; select **Online Content** from the list on the left. Check the **Show content and links from Microsoft Office Online** box and click **OK**. Click **OK** again to close the **Options** dialog box. This change will not take effect until Publisher is restarted.*

Actions:

1. On a blank publication, click the **Picture Frame** button, and select **Clip Art**. The **Insert Clip Art Task Pane** opens.

2. Type in **animals** in the **Search text** box.

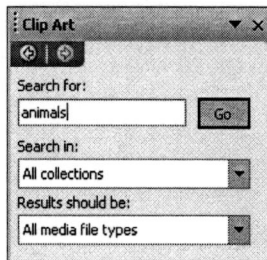

3. Click the **Go** button to see some graphics from this category.

continued over

Exercise 46 - Continued

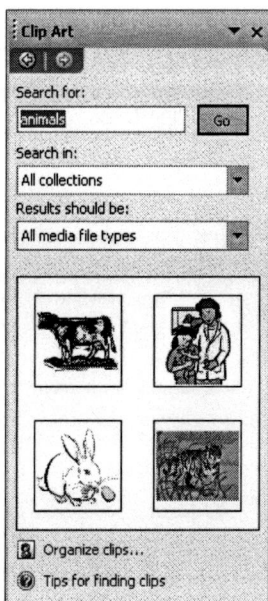

4. The **Task Pane** has navigation buttons, similar to a web browser. To see the previous **Task Pane** used, click the **Back** button, 🔲.

5. Use the **Forward** button, 🔲, to move back to the **animal** search results.

6. Carry out some other searches to see a range of available graphics.

7. Leave the **Clip Art Task Pane** open for the next exercise.

Exercise 47 - Inserting and Deleting Pictures

Guidelines:

The quickest way to insert a graphic is by dragging it from the **Clip Art** window, although there are alternative methods, three of which are used below.

Actions:

1. Using the publication created in the previous exercise, carry out a search to find **Cartoon** graphics.

2. Click on the graphic below, and holding down the mouse, drag it out of the dialog box and on to the page. Click away from the picture to deselect it.

Note: Alternatively, left click just once on the image to insert it onto the page, and move to your desired location by holding down the left mouse button.

3. Delete the search text from the **Task Pane**.

4. Search for **Nature** related graphics and find the **Cloud** picture opposite.

5. Click on the arrow to the right of the **Cloud** picture and select **Insert**.

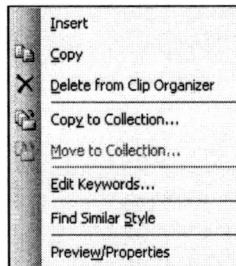

6. Select the **Cloud** picture and press **<Delete>**. The picture disappears.

7. Close the **Clip Art Task Pane** and close the publication without saving.

Exercise 48 - Importing a Picture

Guidelines:

Another way to add a picture to a publication is to insert a picture file. The correct name for this is **importing**.

Actions:

1. Using a blank publication, select the **Picture Frame Tool**, and select **Picture from File**.

2. At the top left side of the page, click and drag a picture frame to display the **Insert Picture** dialog box.

3. Make sure the **Look in** box shows the location where the data files are saved and the **Files of type** box shows **All Picture Formats** (pictures can be saved in several different formats).

4. Click once on the file named **Ostrich**.

5. Click **Insert** to import the file. The frame changes shape, if necessary, to maintain the proportions of the picture.

6. Leave the publication open for the next exercise.

Exercise 49 - Moving and Resizing Pictures

Guidelines:

Picture frames can be moved about the page and resized in the same way as any other object.

Actions:

1. The **Ostrich** picture will be on screen from the previous exercise.

2. Make sure it is selected, i.e. the handles are displayed.

3. Move the cursor over the bottom edge of the picture until the **Move** helpful pointer is displayed.

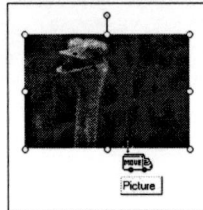

4. Drag the picture down to the middle of the page.

5. Increase the size of the picture, but keep it in proportion, by using a corner handle and dragging it outwards.

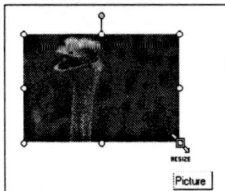

6. Close the publication <u>without</u> saving.

Exercise 50 - Picture Borders

Guidelines:

Pictures or **Clip Art** can be given a border in any colour or thickness to help it to stand out in the publication.

Actions:

1. On a blank publication insert the **Bear** picture from the data provided.

2. Move the cursor over the edge of the picture.

3. Double click on the edge of the picture. The **Format Picture** dialog box is displayed, select the **Colors and Lines** tab.

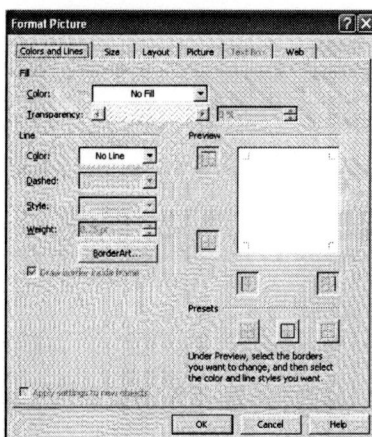

4. Change the **Line Color** to **Orange** and select the **2pt** thickness. Click **OK**. An orange border appears around the picture.

5. This time double click on the middle of the picture. The **Insert Picture** dialog box is displayed.

6. Any picture now selected will replace the original.

7. Click on **Ostrich** and then **Insert**. The **Bear** picture is overwritten.

8. Move the **Ostrich** picture to make sure that the **Bear** picture is not underneath it.

9. Close the publication without saving the changes.

Exercise 51 - Pictures and Text

Guidelines:

More than likely you will want to have text and picture frames on the same page. So that one frame does not overlap another, text will usually wrap around the picture. If however, frames are covered by others, they can be thought of as being in a pile and one can be brought in front of or sent behind another.

Actions:

1. On a blank publication, draw a text box that fills the top half of the page.

2. Insert the text file **Meadowdene**.

3. Zoom in.

4. Display the **Clip Art Task Pane**.

5. In the **Search for** section, select the existing text and type in **farm**.

6. Press **<Enter>** to perform the search.

*Note: Depending on the selection of **Clip Art** available on the computer, other images may be retrieved by this search.*

continued over

Exercise 51 - Continued

7. Select the **agriculture, barns, buildings** clip and insert it into your publication.

8. Close the **Clip Art Task Pane**.

9. Notice that the text has immediately wrapped around the picture.

10. With the farm picture selected, click the **Send to Back** button, , on the **Standard Toolbar** (you may need to click the drop down arrow to see this button).

11. The picture is displayed behind the text (**overlay**), although the handles are still visible. Note that the text is no longer wrapped around the picture. The picture frame is "behind" the text box.

12. Click the **Bring to Front** button, , using the drop down arrow. The farm reappears.

13. Select the text box. Click . Again the farm frame is "behind" the text box.

14. Send the text box to the back.

15. Click on the middle of the farm picture and move it about the text. Note how the text readjusts itself so that it still wraps around the picture.

16. When you are satisfied with the position, draw a text box at the bottom and add your name.

17. Print a copy.

18. Close the publication without saving.

Exercise 52 - Revision

1.   Open the publication **CIA**.

2.   Insert the **Bear** picture from the data provided.

3.   Move it to the top of the text box.

4.   Close the publication <u>without</u> saving.

Exercise 53 - Revision

1.   Open a blank publication.

2.   Open the **Clip Art Task Pane** and search for clips of **books**.

3.   Choose one and insert it.

4.   Change the orientation of the publication to **Landscape**.

5.   Resize the box to fill the page.

6.   Close the publication <u>without</u> saving.

Exercise 54 - Revision

1.   Open a blank publication.

2.   Insert the **Euro** symbol **Clip Art** into a box - it can be found using the search **symbols**.

3.   Close the **Clip Art Task Pane**.

4.   Double click on the picture.

5.   Search using **symbols** again.

6.   Replace the picture with the **Pound** symbol.

7.   Place a **2pt red** border around the picture.

8.   Close the publication <u>without</u> saving.

Exercise 55 - Revision

1. Open the publication **Housewarming**.

2. Double click on the picture of the house and replace it with a different one.

3. Move the picture to another position that does not interfere with any of the text.

4. Place a **2pt black** border around the picture.

5. Change the names to **Barry and Liz**.

6. Close the publication <u>without</u> saving.

Note: *Check the sample publication in* **Answers** *at the end of the guide.*

Exercise 56 - Revision

1. On a blank publication, draw a large text box and insert the text file **Byron**.

2. Make the text **Best Fit** the box.

3. Insert the **quill** picture from the data files into your publication.

4. Enlarge the picture until it is about double its original size.

5. Resize the text box and move the picture frame to the centre of the right side of the box, so that the text wraps to the left of the picture.

6. Print a copy.

7. Close the publication <u>without</u> saving.

Note: *Check the sample publication in* **Answers** *at the end of the guide.*

Section 6

Templates

By the end of this Section you should be able to:

Save Templates
Use Templates

Exercise 57 - Creating a New Template

Guidelines:

Any publication can be set up to use as a template, i.e. a base from which other publications can be generated. *Publisher* has many templates already provided, you have already come across them while using the **New Publication Task Pane**. A **template** can have text or pictures already added so that if several people needed to use the same template, then you can be sure that they are starting from the same point.

Once a template is saved, it can be used at any time to produce a publication. Templates are saved in a special place where they can all be kept together and used by anyone. They can, of course, be saved to any drive or disk, but would then not be available for general use.

Actions:

1. On a blank publication, draw a text box that stretches from margin to margin and is approximately **2cms** deep. You can check this by holding down <Shift> and dragging the vertical ruler on to the page until it is over the box. You will need to zoom in to see the divisions on the ruler.

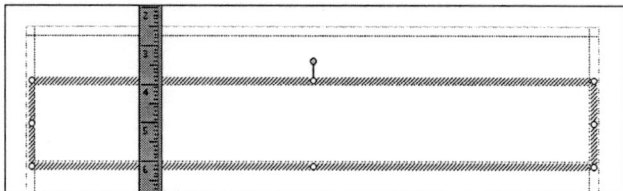

2. Move the ruler out again and enter the text **Meadowdene Weekly** into the box.

3. **Best Fit** the text and **centre** it.

4. Draw a **1pt blue** border around the box.

5. At the bottom of the page, draw another text box, between the margins, this time about **1.5cms** high. Enter the text **Published by** and press <Enter> (if **Text in Overflow** appears make the box slightly larger).

6. On the second line of the box enter the text **Date of Publication**.

7. Once again place a **1pt blue** border around the box.

8. Zoom out so that you can see both boxes on the page. Draw another text box that neatly fits between the two.

continued over

Exercise 57 - Continued

9.   Format this box so that it has **2** columns with a spacing of **0.95cm**.

10. With the column box still selected, fully justify the text (even though there isn't any yet).

11. Insert a suitable **Clip Art** picture so that it overlaps both columns.

12. Place a **1pt green** border around the picture.

13. This forms the basis of the template and should look something like that alongside.

14. The template is now ready for all the week's news to be entered once it has been saved.

15. Select **File | Save as**. At the dialog box, drop down the **Save as type** list and select **Publisher Template**.

16. Notice how the **Save in** location has automatically changed to **Templates**. This is the place that all templates are stored.

Note: In the assessment you may be required to save the template to floppy disk. To do this, select the floppy disk drive from Save in after changing Save as type to Publisher Template.

17. In the **File name** box enter **Weekly** and click **Save**. The template is now saved for repeated use.

18. Close the publication.

Exercise 58 - Using an Existing Template

Guidelines:

Once a template has been created it can be accessed at any time and resaved just like any other publication.

Actions:

1. Select **File | New**. This will display the **New Publication Task Pane**.

2. Click **Templates** underneath the **New from a design** list. The **Weekly Template** is displayed.

Note: *If you cannot see the template, the **Templates** folder may be hidden. Click the **Start** button on the **Taskbar** and then **My Computer**. From the **Menu Bar**, select **Tools | Folder Options** and the **View** tab. From the **Advanced settings** area, scroll down and make sure that **Show hidden files and folders** is checked. Click **OK** and close the **My Computer** window.*

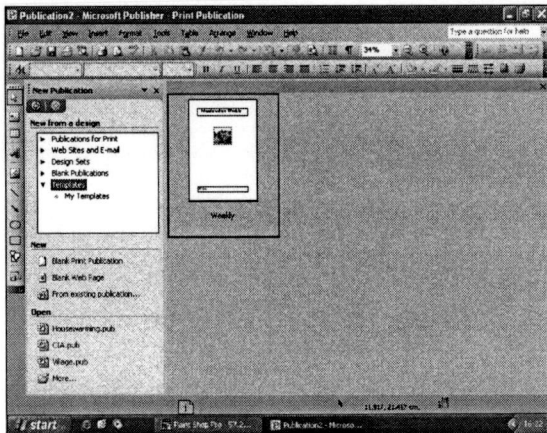

3. Click on the template you have just created.

4. The design you just created is now on screen. However, note that the blue **Title Bar** shows **(Publication2)**, just as all of the blank publications have been.

5. Insert the text file **Meadowdene** into the column box.

6. Increase the font of the imported text to **20pt**.

continued over

Exercise 58 - Continued

7. In the lower box, insert your name after **Published by** and today's date after **Date of Publication**.

8. Save the publication as **Meadowdene Weekly** and print a copy.

9. Close the publication.

*Note: Check the sample publication in **Answers** at the end of the guide.*

Exercise 59 - Deleting a Template

Guidelines:

When templates are no longer required they can be deleted from the list.

Actions;

1. Select **File | Open** to display the **Open Publication** dialog box.

2. From **Look in**, select the template location (**Local Disk (C:)\Documents and Settings\User name\Application Data\Microsoft\Templates**).

*Note: If the template has been saved in a different location, e.g. floppy disk, select the correct location from **Look in**.*

3. Select your template **Weekly**.

4. Press **<Delete>**.

5. At the dialog box select **Yes**.

Confirm File Delete

Are you sure you want to send 'Weekly.pub' to the Recycle Bin?

Yes   No

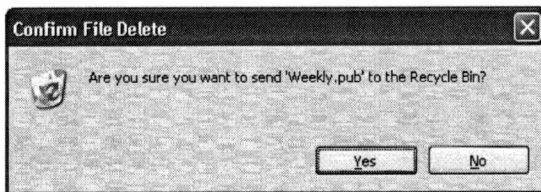

6. The template is deleted. **Cancel** the **Open Publication** dialog box.

Exercise 60 - Revision

1. Open a blank publication and recreate the publication below:

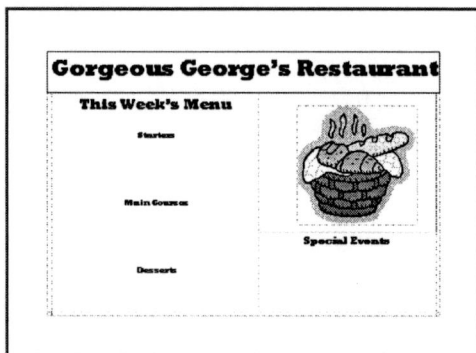

2. Do not worry about using the same font as long as the sizes are compatible.

3. Save this publication as a **Template** called **Menu**.

4. Close the publication.

Exercise 61 - Revision

1. Open the **Template Menu**.

2. Add the following starters to the list: **Soup of the Day** and **Country Pate**.

3. The main courses are **Steak and Chips** and **Bacon, Egg and Chips**. The desserts are **Treacle Sponge and Custard** or **Sticky Toffee Pudding**.

4. In **Special Events** enter the following: **Enter George's eat a pie for charity competition. Ask George for details**.

5. Save the publication as **George** and close it.

Exercise 62 - Revision

1. Locate the **Menu** template. Delete it.

2. Close *Publisher*.

Answers

Exercise 44 - Revision

Chez Charlotte
Menu

Entrées

Pâté
Green salad
Soup of the Day

Main Meals

Frogs' legs
Snails in garlic butter
Boeuf Bourguignon
Chicken Forestière
Wild mushroom omelette
Steak and French fries
Cassoulet

Desserts

Dairy ice cream
Profiteroles
Black Forest gateau
Crème brulée
Sorbet

Exercise 45 - Revision

History of Meadowdene

Exercise 55 - Revision

Exercise 56 - Revision

Exercise 58

Meadowdene Weekly

History of Meadowdene

Meadowdene has been a village community since at least the eleventh century, when it was recorded in the Domesday Book. Stonemasons and carpenters from the village worked on the nearby cathedral. Meadowdene was a Royalist stronghold during the Civil War and still has royal connections, as the King walks his poodles in the local forest. Today, we have a thriving organic farming industry and a new vineyard, opened last year by Henry Bottle and Sons seems to be doing well.

Next week, we would like to publish a feature on the allegedly haunted folly, at the south side of the forest. Please get in touch if you have any interesting stories. There are lots of forthcoming events in the next few months. If you are organizing, or know of an event, contact Phil as soon as possible.

Glossary

Best Fit	A setting that will adjust the font size within a text frame so that all the text fits exactly into the available area.
Catalog	A collection of pre-prepared layouts, upon which new publications may be based.
Clip Gallery	A feature that gives access to the collection of **Clip Art** available within *Office*.
Colour Separation Proof	A printout where each colour used is printed on a separate page.
Composite Proof	A print out showing all items placed on a page.
Font	A type or style of print.
Handles	The black squares that are displayed at the corners and at the centre of the sides of an object when it is selected.
Import	To insert text or pictures, which already exist in another location, into a publication.
Indent	An amount by which text is moved towards the vertical centre line of a page, away from a margin.
Justified	An alignment setting which straightens both the left and right margins of the text.
Layout	The arrangement of a publication to suit various purposes; **Special Fold** card, **Label**, **Envelope**, etc.
Layout Guides	Blue dotted lines around the page, which can help to line up objects on the page.
Margin Guides	Indicate the boundaries of the printed page.
Object	An item within a publication such as a picture, or a text box
Objects Toolbar	An extra toolbar, that by default is positioned down the left side of the screen, enabling the creation of various objects on the page.
Orientation	Whether the page is arranged on its side or upright.
Page Setup	A facility that allows the layout and orientation of a publication to be specified.
Picture Frame	A frame that restricts the area in which a graphic image can be positioned and/or viewed.

Point	A unit of measurement of font size. 1 point equals 1/72 inch.
Publication	The universal name for a finished file created within *Publisher*.
Sans Serif	A style of font that does not have any decorative lines or curls on the "stalks" of letters.
Select	To highlight a section of text or click on an object to identify it for editing or formatting.
Serif	A style of font that has decorative lines or curls on the "stalks" of letters.
Taskbar	By default, a grey band across the bottom of the **Desktop**, which displays a button for each program that is currently running.
Template	A ready-made publication that requires only the text to be edited or a picture to be changed.
Text Frame	A frame that restricts the area in which text can be typed and/or viewed.
Text Wrapping	The way text "flows" around a picture or other object positioned inside a text frame.
Wizard	A step-by-step sequence of options that allows a user to customise a finished publication to their own requirements.
Zoom	A function that allows the degree of magnification of a page to be adjusted to suit the user.

Index

Record of Achievement Matrix

This Matrix is to be used to measure your progress while working through the guide. This is a self assessment process, you judge when you are competent. Remember that afterwards there is an assessment to test your competence.

Tick boxes are provided for each feature. 1 is for no knowledge, 2 is for some knowledge and 3 is for competent. A section is only complete when column 3 is completed for all parts of the section.

Tick the Relevant Boxes **1**: No Knowledge **2**: Some Knowledge **3**: Competent

Section	No	Exercise	1	2	3
1 Fundamentals	1	Starting Publisher			
	2	Using a Wizard			
	3	Closing a Publication			
	4	Creating a Blank Publication			
	5	The Publisher Screen			
	6	Text Boxes and Entering Text			
	7	Zoom			
	8	Closing Publisher			
2 Publications	13	Saving a Publication			
	14	Opening a Publication			
	15	Cursor Movement			
	16	Selecting Text			
	17	Editing Text			
	18	Page Setup			
	19	Setting Margins and Layout Guides			
	20	Printing			
3 Text Formatting	26	Changing Fonts and Text Size			
	27	Alignment			
	28	Paragraph Formatting			
4 Working With Boxes	32	Text Box Properties			
	33	Moving and Resizing Boxes			
	34	Using Best Fit			
	35	Applying Borders and Lines			
	36	Line Formatting			
	37	Importing Text Files			
	38	Columns			
	39	Column Spacing			
5 Pictures	46	The Clip Gallery			
	47	Inserting and Deleting Pictures			
	48	Importing a Picture			
	49	Moving and Resizing Pictures			
5 Pictures	50	Picture Borders			
	51	Pictures and Text			
6 Templates	57	Creating a New Template			
	58	Using an Existing Template			
	59	Deleting a Template			

Other Products from CiA Training

If you have enjoyed using this guide you can obtain other products from our range of over 100 titles. CiA Training Ltd is a leader in developing self-teach training materials and courseware.

Open Learning Guides

Teach yourself by working through them in your own time. Our range includes products for: Windows, Word, Excel, Access, Works, PowerPoint, Project, Lotus 123, Lotus Word Pro, Internet, FrontPage and many more... We also have a large back catalogue of products, including PageMaker, Quattro Pro, Paradox, Ami Pro, etc. please call for details.

ECDL & ECDL Advanced

We produce accredited training materials for the European Computer Driving Licence (ECDL) qualification, for both the Standard and Advanced syllabus. In 2001 we became one of the first companies in the world to obtain accreditation for the ECDL Advanced modules.

CLAIT Plus

Have you enjoyed doing New CLAIT? Well why not go one step further and take the CLAIT Plus qualification. Materials are now available which follow the same format as our successful New CLAIT material.

e-Quals

To follow the success of our other resources, we have further expanded the courseware portfolio to include training materials for the City & Guilds e-Quals qualification. Specifically designed to steer the user around the features needed to pass the e-Quals assessments.

Trainer's Packs

Specifically written for use with tutor led I.T. courses. The trainer is supplied with a trainer guide (step by step exercises), course notes (for delegates), consolidation exercises (for use as reinforcement) and course documents (course contents, pre-course questionnaires, evaluation forms, certificate template, etc). All supplied on CD with the rights to edit and copy the documents.

Purchasing Options

The above publications are available in a variety of purchasing options; as single copies, class sets and or site licences. However, Trainer's Packs are only available as site licences.

Conventional Tutor Led Training

CiA have been successfully delivering classroom based I.T. training throughout the UK since 1985. New products are constantly being developed; please call to be included on our mailing list. Information about all these materials can be viewed at www.ciatraining.co.uk.

© CiA Training Ltd 2004

Notes

Notes

Notes